Official Proclamation Of Real Moorish American Nationality

Our Status And Jurisdiction As Citizens Of The U.S.A.

Black & White Edition
Prepared for Public Distribution

© 2014

The Ali Shuffle

Peter Moon, *The Montauk Book of the Dead* (2005)

At the current time, the door to Moorish mysteries is opening far and wide. The Age of Pisces is at an end, and the Moors are coming to receive their inheritance. Drew Ali instigated this process when he returned to America and released a publication known as the Circle Seven Koran. While Drew Ali did not deliver the concise formula as was clearly delineated in Synchronicity and the Seventh Seal, he represented the energy and was the energy of such. Drew Ali was very much a part of the mythos and reality that enabled me to write that book. What Drew Ali wrote was geared towards a format that would be accepted by his people at that particular time. It apparently worked quite well.

When the Moorish Science reached its peak in 1929, it was on the heels of one of the greatest, but most dangerous, discoveries Drew Ali ever made. In 1928, Ali attended a Pan American conference in Havana Cuba where he enjoyed broad recognition from a host of other countries. They were, of course, recognizing his sovereign status as a Moorish national who was representing the ancient empire of Amexem. Keep in mind that other countries had no reason to fear Drew Ali or what he represented. It was at this conference, however, that he received a document which was to change the face of Moorish Science forever and would eventually lead to what is known as the Great Schism. That is the name the Moorish community uses to refer to the dispersal of Moorish Science into different groups.

The document Drew Ali received was a copy of a mandate whereby the Amexem Empire extended a land grant of the entire Western Hemisphere to certain Europeans. I have not yet seen the document, and its exact contents are highly mysterious, yet its ramifications literally turned the United States of America upside down. Essentially, it "leased" America to a certain party for a particular number of years, not unlike the way China leased Hong Kong to Great Britain, The lease was up in 2004.

It is entirely reasonable to believe that such a document, if it still exists and can be brought to light, is a mere relic of a long forgotten era that has no significant meaning in today's legal system. That would be fine except for one very important point. If you have truly studied the detailed legal history of the United States of America, you would understand that there is more than a little truth to the prospect of their being such a document. Why? The entire legal history of the United States is predicated on such a proposition.

What is known is that Secretary of State Hughes, from the U.S. Government, attended the Pan American conference and was made privy to this mandate. So were several other heads of state. As a result, a closed-door conference between several nations was held in Geneva, Switzerland and a labyrinthine series of discussions and negotiations began. The Geneva conferences went on for some five years, but records are still kept sealed to this very day. It is known that several international banks called in their loans as a result of this potential legal threat and the stock market crashed in 1929. Several countries, which included the United States, Portugal, France, and Spain, declared bankruptcy in order that relevant powers could buffer themselves from any potential legal claims.

In the case of the United States of America, it was reorganized with a new corporate legal status. Franklin Roosevelt was part and parcel of the entire plan when he abolished the gold standard and created the New Deal. Federal Reserve notes were then issues in place of gold-backed currency. The Great Seal of the Moors was used on the back of the notes.

People behind the Geneva conferences were so concerned about any potential boomerangs from the Moorish issue that they began a full barreled character assassination of Moorish heritage. The most flagrant example of this was when two Master Masons put together the infamous Amos and Andy show and it became the first nationally syndicated radio show in history. It was deliberately designed to spoof the Moorish Science Temple by lampooning them as the "Mystic Order of the Knights of the Sea" and callously referred to them as sardines. From one perspective, this can be viewed as hysterically funny, especially when you consider that the dignitaries were given titles such as the Swordfish, the Mackerel, and the Kingfish. On the other hand, it was a deliberate and malicious act of intent designed to portray any Moor as the most laughable example of what could be termed the lowest common denominator. Not long after Amos and Andy had its national debut, Drew Ali was arrested and mysteriously died. This has been ignored by both history and conspiracy books. When you see how integrally connected the Moors are to the history of the world, let alone the United States, you see that they are a guidepost to the true history of the planet. This is the lamp of illumination, the Hermit's lamp (from the Tarot), that the secret societies have long played tribute to in their writings.

By reason of our social conditioning, it seems utterly preposterous that the old Moorish Empire could have an actual court-of-law legal claim on this country. Conversely, it appears that world leaders have been deathly afraid of such and have even prepared themselves to legally avoid the inevitable. Once again, the Moors show themselves to be hard-wired into the infrastructure of our consciousness as well as the historical paper trail.

September 29, 2014

Letter from Lead Editor

Islam,

I rise giving all perfect praise to Allah, His Prophet in these days, Noble Drew Ali, and the forerunner, Marcus Mosiah Garvey El. In the spirit of Love, Truth, Peace, Freedom, and Justice, I greet you.

In 1928, El Hajj Sharif Abdul Ali, known to the world as Noble Drew Ali, attended the Pan-American Conference in Havana, Cuba. At said conference, also attended by the not-invited Secretary of State for the UNITED STATES OF AMERICA, our Prophet received from the nations of America the mandate recognizing the Moor's claim to the Americas, and simultaneously, the expiration of the European mandate to occupy Moorish lands in the Western Hemisphere. As the USA's first victim of COINTELPRO, our Prophet returned to the states to find his temple in turmoil, which indirectly led to his transition from this world. As known to the Moors, receipt of this Mandate directly resulted in the US stock market crash that occurred less than a year later---the nations of the Earth complicit in the denial of Moorish nationality knew they had best pull out of the system before everything on the North American landmass could be nationalized, including their ill-gotten assets and interests.

Before his transition, our Prophet warned the Moors at that time they would not realize what was brought to them for at least 50 years---not coincidentally, this 50-year mark was the decade that produced the Moors currently most active in ensuring the Prophet has his way, including myself. Our Prophet ensured that, once the Moors finally came into their own around the year 2000 (when most of us had reached the age of majority) and woke up to the realization of who they were, all they would have to do is wake up and carry out his law.

Our Prophet was right in exact in his statement that one day, the Moors would LOVE him. When one realizes what is was he brought to his people and how it was delivered unto him, the seeing and knowing cannot help but appreciate the Prophet's absolute genius. To prevent its suppression, the Mandate was included as the opening section of the Holy Koran of the Moorish Holy Temple of Science Circle 7, where it is protected by the religious freedoms codified in the statutes of the UNITED STATES. The seal of our nation can be found on the one fiat debt note our Prophet knew we would always have access to: the one "dollar" bill. Those who contest this will be hard pressed to find another national currency with TWO seals, national or otherwise.

The issuance of this Official Proclamation of Real Moorish American Nationality serves as constructive notice to the nations of the world: The Moors are back, and the Judgment of the Nations of the Earth is upon us. Woe to those who would attempt to hinder our Divine and National movement. Honors and may the Blessings of Allah be upon those who assist in our mission to uplift fallen humanity and take our rightful place in the affairs of men.

Your sister in Islam,

Tauheedah Sabreen Najee-Ullah El

Secretary/ Treasurer and Historian
Moorish Science Temple California, Inc.

Managing Editor and C.E.O.
Califa Media®

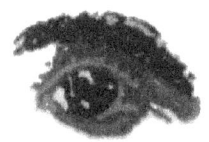

The Moorish Divine and National Movement of North America

Founded by our Prophet, Noble Drew Ali, 1916 A.D.

FROM THE OFFICES OF

The Prophet

and

The Grand Body

OF

The MOORISH SCIENCE TEMPLE OF AMERICA

Incorporated 1926 A.D.

OFFICIAL

PROCLAMATION

OF REAL

MOORISH AMERICAN NATIONALITY

OUR STATUS AND JURISDICTION AS

Citizens of the U.S.A.

The Moorish American National

Statement of Facts

Notice: A Divine Warning by the Prophet for the Nations

Averment of Jurisdiction

Moorish American Proclamation of Free National Status and Jurisdiction

Proclamation of Status

Our Authority

Moorish American Proclamation of Birthrights of Religious Autonomy

Prophet Makes a Plea to the Nation

Divine Constitution and By-Laws of the Moorish Science Temple of America

Proclaimed members of the Moorish Science Temple of America and Citizens of the U.S.A.

Moorish Leader's Historical Message to America

Public Notice

To: Every State, County, and Local Tribunal, of the Honorable United States of America and Supreme Court and Congress; The International Court of Justice, all Free National Governments under their Free National Constitution, Republics, Monarchies, Family of Nations, Indigenous People of the Earth and the World's Sovereign Orders of The Book, e.g. Hindu, Hebrew, Christian, Moslem; and every Country, Kingdom, Indigenous Tribes and All Members of the Human Family, et.al.

A Divine Warning by The Prophet
For the Nations

The citizens of all free national governments according to their national constitution are all one family bearing one free national name. Those who fail to recognize the free national name of their constitutional government are classed as undesirables, and are subject to all inferior names, abuses, mistreatments that the citizens care to bestow upon them. And it is a sin for any group of people to violate the national constitutional laws of a free national government and cling to names and the principles that delude to slavery.

I, the Prophet, was prepared by the Great God Allah to warn my people to repent from their sinful ways and go back to that state of mind of their forefathers' Divine and national principles that they will be law-abiders and receive their divine rights as citizens, according to the free national constitutional that was prepared for all free national beings. They are to claim their own free national name and religion. There is but one issue for them to be recognized by this government and nations of the earth and that comes only through the connection of the Moorish Divine National Movement, which is incorporated in this government and recognized by all other nations of the world. And through it they and their children can receive their Divine rights, unmolested by other citizens that they can cast a free national ballot at the polls under the free national constitution of the States Government and not under a granted privilege as has been the existing condition for many generations.

You who doubt whether I, the Prophet, and my principles are right for the redemption of my people, go to those who know the law, in the City Hall and among the officials in your government and ask them under an intelligent tone, and they will be glad to render you a favorable reply, for they are glad to see me bring you out of darkness into light. Money doesn't make the man; it is free national standards and power that make the man and the nation. The wealth of all national governments, gold, silver and commerce belong to the citizens alone and without your national citizenship by name and principles, you have no true wealth, and I am hereby calling on all true citizens that stand for a National Free Government, and the enforcement of the constitution to help me in my missionary work because I need all support from all true American citizens of the United States of America. Help me to save my people who have fallen from the constitutional laws of the government. I am depending on your support to get them back to the constitutional fold again that they will learn to love instead of hate and will live according to Love, Truth, Peace, Freedom and Justice, supporting our free national constitution of the United States of America.

I love my people and desire their unity and mine back to their own free National and Divine standard because day by day they have been violating the national and constitutional laws of their government by claiming names and principles that are unconstitutional. If Italians, Greeks, English, Chinese, Japanese, Turks, and Arabians are forced to proclaim their free national name and religion before the constitutional government of the United States of America, it is no more than right that the law should be enforced upon all other American citizens alike. In all other governments when a man is born and raised there and asked for his national descent name and if he fails to give it, he is misused, imprisoned, or exiled. Any group of people that fail to answer up to the constitutional standards of law by name and principles, because to be a citizen of any government you must claim your national descent name. Because they place their trust upon issue and names formed by their forefathers.

The word Negro deludes in the Latin language to the word nigger; the same as the word "colored" deludes to anything that is painted, varnished and dyed. And every nation must bear a national descent name of their forefathers, because honoring thy fathers and thy mothers, your days will be lengthened upon this earth. These names have never been recognized by any true American citizens of this day. Through your free national name you are known and recognized by said national government in which you live. The 14th and 15th Amendments brought the North and South in unit, placing the Southerners who were at that time without power with the constitutional body of power. And at that time, 1865, the free national constitutional law that was enforced since 1774 declared all men equal and free and if all men are declared by the free national constitution to be free and equal since that constitution has never changed, there is no need for the application of the 14th and 15th Amendments for the salvation of our people and citizens.

So, there isn't but one supreme issue for my people to use to redeem that which was lost, and that is through the above statements. Then the lion and the lamb can lie down together in yonder hills. And neither will be harmed, because Love, Truth, Peace, Freedom and Justice will be reigning in this land. In those days the United States will be one of the greatest civilized and prosperous governments of the world, but if the above principles are not carried out by the citizens and my people in this government, the worst is yet to come because the Great God of the Universe is not pleased with the works that are being performed in North America by my people and this great sin must be removed from the land to save it from the enormous earthquakes, disease, etc.

And I, the Prophet, do hereby believe that this administration of the government being more wisely prepared by more genius citizens that believe in their free national constitution and laws through the help of such classes of citizens. I, the Prophet, truly believe that my people will find the true and Divine ways of their forefathers, and learn to stop serving the carnal customs and merely ideas of man, that have never done them any good, but have always harmed them.

So, I the Prophet, am hereby calling aloud with a Divine plea to all true American citizens to help me remove this great sin which has been committed and is being practiced by my people in the United States of America because they know it is not the true and Divine way, without understanding that they had fallen from the true light into utter darkness of sin, and there is not a nation on earth today that will recognize them socially, religiously, politically or economically, etc. In their present condition of their endeavors in which they themselves try to force upon a civilized world, they will not refrain from their sinful ways of action and their deeds have brought Jim Crow-ism, segregation, and everything that brings harm to human beings on earth. And they fought the Southerners for all these great misuses, but I have traveled in the South and have examined conditions there, and it is the works of my people continuously practicing the things which bring dishonor, disgrace, and disrespect to any nation that lives the life. And I am hereby calling on all true American citizens for moral support and finance to help me in my great missionary work to bring my people out of darkness into marvelous light.

-FROM THE PROPHET

Prophet Noble Drew Ali

MOORISH SCIENCE TEMPLE OF AMERICA)) Petitioner)) _____)) UNITED STATES OF AMERICA) UNITED STATES CONGRESS) UNITED STATES SUPREME COURT))) Respondents)	**AVERMENT OF JURISDICTION**

NOW COMES THE PETITIONER, THE MOORISH SCIENCE TEMPLE OF AMERICA, AND ORIGINAL CONSTITUTIONAL LAW ENFORCE IN 1774 TO MOVE THIS AVERMENT OF JURISDICTION TO THE STATUS OF THE MOORISH AMERICANS HEREBY CHALLENGE THE RESPONDENT, THE UNITED STATES, THE UNITED STATES CONGRESS, UNITED STATES SUPREME COURT, ET AL., TO BE RECEIVED AS THE ORDER OF TODAY'S JUDICIAL BUSINESS: THE SUPREME LAWS OF THE UNITED STATES AND ALL OTHER FREE NATIONAL GOVERNMENTS JUDICIALLY UPHOLD, THERE CAN BE NO LEGAL PROCEEDING WITHOUT THE ESTABLISHMENT OF PROPER STATUS AND CORRECT JURISDICTION. THESE TWO PILLARS OF LAW MUST BE IN PLACE AND HAVE PRECEDENCE BEFORE THE ADJUDICATION OF ALL FORMAL AND ALLEGED OFFENSES CAN BE ADDRESSED.

Cited Supreme Court Decisions, Presidential Pardons, and Acts of Congress

- TREATY OF PEACE OF 1786

- LOUISIANA PURCHASE TREATY – 1805

- PRESIDENTIAL PARDON OF ABDUL RAHMAN IBRAHIMI – 1828

- AMISTAD MUTINY OF 1841

- TREATY OF GUADALUPE HIDALGO 1848

- DRED SCOTT DECISION OF 1856

- EXPATRIATION ACT OF 1868

The above cited Supreme Court Decisions, combined in resolves as "Dred Scott vs. The Laws and Citizens of the United States," were the lawful gnosis personifying the Supreme Issues of Status and Jurisdiction: these issues are relevant to the immediate matters of Nationality and Manumissions of the indigenous Moorish to the Continental breast of North America.

Hear now the greatest bounds of jurisdiction, empowered to the wisdom in The Supreme Court of The United States, is now challenged to render, in written Personam its Constitutional Jurisdiction to govern the lost-found Aboriginal Tribes of the Moorish American Nation, an estimated sixty million descendants. The U.S. Supreme Court in full authority to exercise the power of The United States Constitution, joined with the entire Embodiments of Congress, now have the burden of proof to any jurisdiction to justly govern the Clean and Pure Nation of Moorish Americans present in their Proper Person now before you.

The uniting of this Nation is the calling of our family, bearing their one free national name of Moorish American, is not being misconstrued as a Religious Organization confined to The United States First Amendment nor to be confused with those "Persons" denationalized in the United States Fourteenth Amendment under the ex post facto Slave labels of Negroes, Blacks, and Colored People. When after no Jurisdiction over the Moorish Americans can be claimed and proven by the challenged sovereignty whether spiritually, ancestrally, indigenously, politically or legally, then both The Lion and The Lamb are to lay together and neither will be harmed in this New Era. They are to let the Peace be still in the North American Continent and the World, now and forever.

Now, the highest Court in the United States, being in want of said jurisdiction and therefore without power to issue an 'In Personam Judgment.' We, the Free National Americans with our Seals affixed here upon, do hereby declare the autonomy of our Moorish American Nation. Our first inalienable Right to be Free, to be ourselves, God-like, in his likeness and image.

The Moorish American National

Moorish American Flag

Seal of the Moorish Divine National Movement

Moorish American Real Proclamation of Free National Status and Jurisdiction

Holy Koran of the M.S.T. of A.

Ch. 47 v. 15
"The time has come that every nation must worship under its own vine and fig tree, and every tongue must confess his own."

Now, in accordance with the Divine Plan of the Ages, it is mandatory for the people, standing in their Proper Person, to proclaim their Free National Status, thus dissolving all unauthorized political bonds and assumed jurisdictions.

Ch. 45 v. 1-2
"The fallen sons and daughters of the Asiatic Nation of North America need to learn to love instead of hate; and to know of his higher self and lower self. This is the uniting of the Holy Koran of Mecca for teaching and instructing all Moorish Americans etc."

"The key to civilization was and is in the hands of the Asiatic nations. The Moorish, who were the ancient Moabites, and the founders of the Holy City of Mecca."

Ch. 47 v. 6-8
"The Moabites from the land of Moab who received permission from the Pharaohs of Egypt to settle and inhabit North West Africa; they were the founders and are the true possessors of the present Moroccan Empire. With their Canaanite, Hittite and Amorite brethren who sojourned from the land of Canaan seeking homes."

"The River Nile was drudged and made by the ancient Pharaohs of Egypt in order to trade with the surrounding kingdoms. Also the Niger River was drudged by the great Pharaoh of Egypt in those ancient days for trade, and it extends eastward from the River Nile, westward across the Atlantic. It was used for trade and transportation."

Real Proclamation of Status

Ch. 47 v. 9-13

"According to all true and divine records of the human race, there is no negro, black, or colored race attached to the human family, because all the inhabitants of Africa were and are of the human race, descendants of the ancient Canaanite nation from the holy land of Canaan."

"What your ancient forefathers were, you are today without a doubt of contradiction."

"There is no one who is able to change man from the descendant nature of his forefathers, unless his power extends beyond the great universal Creator Allah Himself."

"These laws are to be strictly preserved by the members of all the Temples, of the Moorish Science Temple of America. That they will learn to open their meetings and guide it according to the principles of Love, Truth, Peace, Freedom and Justice."

Ch. 47 v. 16-17

"Through sin and disobedience every nation has suffered slavery, due to the fact that they honored not the creed and principles of their forefathers."

"That is why the nationality of the Moors was taken from them in 1774 and the words negro, black and colored were given to the Asiatics of America who were of Moorish descent, because they honored not the principles of their mother and father, and strayed after the gods of Europe whom they knew nothing of."

The reason these truths have not been known is because the Moslems had these secrets and kept them back from the outside world, and when the time appointed by Allah they loosened the keys and freed these secrets, and for the first time in ages have these secrets been delivered in the hands of the Moslems of America. All authority and right of this Proclamation of 1927.

By the Prophet
Noble Drew Ali

The industrious acts of the Moslems of northwest and southwest Africa. These are the Moabites, Hamathites and Canaanites, who were driven out of the land of Canaan, by Joshua, and received permission from the Pharaohs of Egypt to settle in that portion of Egypt. In later years they formed themselves kingdoms. These kingdoms are called this day Morocco, Algiers, Tunis, Tripoli, and Mauritania.

The advent of We, the Moorish Americans, were Divinely Ordained forth into rightful existence, in due time, as a Nation, by the will of the Great God at the abolishment of slavery, as ratified by the United States Congressional Thirteenth Amendment in 1865 A.D. this Congressional Manumission of the Sons and Daughters of Africa brought to light a Nation of People upon the Earth. This Nation of West African descendants have now come to lawfully link themselves again with the families of nations and to worship under their own vine and fig tree, which have been the inherited Birthrights of all Men through the descendent nature of their Ancient Forefathers. This is the true inalienable inheritance of every member of the human family and nation upon the Earth. And The Moorish Americans are a part and parcel of the Human Family.

The Moorish Americans are Descendants of Moroccans. The Northwestern Capitol of the Mighty Carthage/ Moorish Empire (700 B.C. – 1820 A.D.), the Ancient Moabites whom inhabited the North Western and South Western shores of Africa, born indigenous in the Continental lands of America. The Moorish Americans are a Clean and Pure Nation. We have naturally derived our Free National Name "Moorish" by West African descent and "American" by indigenous birth.

We now proclaim the heritage of our ancient Forefathers, the ancient Moabites whom are also known as the Mississippian Mound builders, the Califas of California and the Olmecs of Mexico. True records prove the Moorish Americans are the original inhabitants of North America, whether by legacy or dormant conditions of servitude.

We also proclaim as Parcel the Continental American Territories through the blood of our forefathers that has been shed, in acquiring the independence and sustaining the prosperity and tranquility which has glorified the independence of the United Stated of America through all of Her wars and conflicts, defending the principles of the Republic for which She stands.

The new Nation of Moorish Americans, is the fruition of the original 13th Amendment, with its full body of 20 Section, repudiated by the Reconstruction Congress. Now, not to be denied! This right to proclaim our Free National Name before the congressional folds of government, should not be misconstrued as an act of aggression, rebellion, nor declaration of war against the harmony of the United Stated of America, its laws, citizens nor allies. In lieu of inevitable compliance with the natural laws of indigenous comity of nations all over the world, both Ancient and modern, which demands all men to proclaim their nationality.

nationality in order to be recognized and accepted by all other free national governments. We acknowledge the unavoidable destiny of our divine attainment and deliverance to be a Holy People, as undeniable and in due time. The applications of the 14th and 15th Amendments are reconstructed and established forms of Government designed to be destructive to these ends. Six scores and ten years of enforcement of these laws lay bare an unbroken history of iron-hand oppression, which remain unchanged and proven that descendants of West Africans will never be free while woven into the fabric of European Jurisprudence which has threads of European psychology and neocolonialism.

The United States of America, with Her Great Congressional 13th Amendment of 1865, abolished the institution of Slavery, which in fact repealed and did rescind wholly: all Slaves, Slave Masters and Slave Names of said institution. Albeit contrived and did willfully assume Jurisdiction over the comatose, Ex-Slaves and extended its powers, through the Clause 'All Persons Born,' referring solely to reestablishing the institutions of Negro, Black, Colored, Chattel, and other Commercial Properties, as used in the 14th Amendment. This wrongful and willful Act intentionally abused Congressional Powers of a Free National Government and alone buried the Ex-Slave in the shallow grave of Ex Post Facto Laws of its 14th and 15th Amendments. Therefore, today, the U.S. courts through the Several Corporate States still owns and have assumable jurisdiction of all such Denationalized Persons, clearly certified by the States, upon live birth as Negro, Blacks and Colored, etc.

The U.S. 14th Amendment uses the term 'Persons' to defuse the "3/5 clause" of its Constitution (Art. 1-Sec. 3) and was written strictly applicable to slaves and Ex – Slaves, misnomer Negroes, Colored Folks, Black People, etc. Under Color of Law, that document gives the United States clear title and ownership to said persons, as property, and evinces Assumable Jurisdiction over the automatism of fallen humanity.

The 14th Amendment was ratified in full knowledge it would perpetuate all so-called Negroes, as an undeclared and wretched People, to remain alienated and separated from the Human Family. This mandates Ex-Slaves into an unconscious act of Voluntary Enthrallment by clinging to those Names and Principles that delude to slavery. As long as the Ex-Slaves accept the Slave Labels of Negro, Black, and Colored People, that has been Certified upon their decree of live birth by the States wherein they were born, then they will live the life of a Slave, bearing names that delude to slavery, yet not knowing they have been Denationalized to the status of slaves.

Yet neither the Administrative United States nor any other Sovereign power have established lawful jurisdiction over the Clean and Pure Nation of Moorish Americans. Nay, neither written nor assumed, nor will such jurisdiction over the subject matter be surrendered, given or hypothesized. Whereas, the above decree of hostage making can have no jurisdictional bearing upon the Clean and Pure Nation of Moorish Americans. The Administrative United States is now being called forth, with its Congressional powers as handed down in the last Clauses of the Reconstruction Amendments, before the International Bar of Indigenous People and League of United Nations for Human Rights, in light of the full Constitutional Body of Laws and Principles for which it stands, to answer this proper Federal Question and lawful challenge, to demonstrate. The Administrative United States cannot muster adjudication to the above previously submitted National Averment of Jurisdiction.

[signature: Prophet Bey Dbw Ali]

Our Authority

10105905
STATE OF ILLINOIS
COOK COUNTY } SS. NO.
FILED FOR RECORD

1928 AUG 1 PM 2 52

AND RECORDED IN
BOOK _____ PAGE _____

State of Illinois,
County of COOK

I, NOBLE DREW ALI,

do solemnly swear that at a meeting of the members of the MOORISH SCIENCE TEMPLE OF AMERICA held at Chicago in the County of Cook and State of Illinois, on the 20th day of July A.D. 1928, for that purpose, the following persons were appointed Trustees SHEIKS

according to the rules and usages of such MOORISH SCIENCE TEMPLE OF AMERICA

NOBLE DREW ALI, HEALY EL, HALL BEY, LOVETT BEY, AND FOREMAN BEY. The Moorish Science Temple of America deriving its power and authority from the Great Koran of Mohammed to propagate the faith and extend the learning and truth of the Great Prophet of Ali in America. To anoint, appoint and consecrate missionaries of the prophet and to establish the faith of Mohammed in America.

And said MOORISH SCIENCE TEMPLE OF AMERICA adopted as its corporate name, the following MOORISH SCIENCE TEMPLE OF AMERICA

And at said meeting, this affiant acted as Presiding officer.

Subscribed and Sworn to Before me,
_____ day of _____ A.D. 19__

Drew Ali

Linta W. Council
Notary Public

The Moorish American Proclamation of Birthrights and Autonomy

The United Stated in her infancy bears witness that no Nation will be free to live out its Creed, personify the Grand Principles and attain unlimited capacity of development while under the yoke, laws and tyranny of another Government. Neither has the Moorish American been free to be themselves in the 140 years since their emancipation from Negro Chattel Slavery, while under Assumable Jurisdiction of the U.S. 14th and 15th Amendments of the granted privileges, separated from the Rights guaranteed to all free National Citizens in the body of Her Constitution.

The Moorish Americans, through Rights of Divinity, have come forth as a Clean and Pure people, empowered with the inalienable birthright to be an upright, independent and fearless Nation. In accordance with the Declaration of Human Rights, we have the Human Right to be known by one, true, Free National Name, and by number, with Divine Constitution, officials of Government with Attaché and Ambassadors, Principles, Our Flag and Holy Book. We have the inherent Right to lands, air, and waterways originally civilized, inhabited and cultivated by our Ancient Forefathers and to insure the sanctity of our Men, Women, Children and their prosperity.

That to secure these rights there are Governments instituted among people, deriving their just powers from the consent of the governed. That whenever any form of government becomes destructive of these ends, it then becomes the just right of the people to abandon it and to institute a new government, laying its foundations on the Omnipotent Principles of Love, Truth, Peace, Freedom and Justice, and organizing its powers in such form, as to them shall seem most likely to effect their safety and happiness. While man's evils to man are made sufferable, evil is not requisite to man.

To provide new guards for our future security:

All judicial conventions based on the 1868 congressionally ratified 14th Amendment jurisdiction with its intents to recycle slavery congressionally abolished by the ratified 13th Amendment, negligent of status and in want of lawful jurisdiction are hereby declared ex post facto and void of judicial, civil, and divine substance.

Naturalization: the process by which a whole person, in full consciousness of nationality by birth and descent, applies for citizenship, a choice among all free national constitutions, has been politically denied to the ex-slaves. And there has been no record documented, since the enactment of the 13th Amendment, to reflect the naturalization clause by treaty, application, nor judicial hearing, nor petition, nor declaration of allegiance in true intercourse to the Moorish American, of lawful age and be accepted, by choice, as naturalized citizens of the United States. Being Negro, Colored, Black or African American, etc., are not Nationalities that bear one Free National descent name of their forefathers, but used in the semblance thereof. Ergo, the Negro State was never designed to muster the noble status of true Citizenship or qualify the bearers to reach from the Federal Question of "Denationalization" to the choice of Nationalization. The produce thereby is colorable citizenry leaving a residue of mental slavery, which has been the existing condition until now. Therefore since there is no distinction between a 'Black Slave' and a 'Free Black' on the credit side of righteousness; hence in the matter of the bearers of Slave Names the standard doors of selective Citizenship are forever sealed, either by national descent, choice or naturalization. The United States has always known so-called Colored People, that were made exclusively in America and are not Citizens, especially in the judicial affirmation of the Dred Scott decision.

Unconsciously, Moors have used Slave Names, not knowing these labels are unacceptable, without worth and decry muster among the realms of free nationalized citizens; making Blacks, excluding Indians not taxed, as 3/5 of all other "Persons," subjected to perpetual taxation without true representation as those Members under a Free National Descent Name.

High diligence of honor and glory are due for the contributions and accomplishments of our people unjustly siphoned by another then hoisted as their own. Because of this practice, the credibility, trust, and reliance are misplaces.

This component of iron hand oppression is places upon the people who, within the bounds of the U.S. Fourteenth and Fifteenth Amendments, have been denied repatriated Nationhood, and the labor of all their good words, works and deed will glorify their owner. The 14th and 15th Amendments were ratified in full light of the Supreme Court's Dred Scott decision (1856), which declared Denationalized Africans, whether Negro Slave or freed Negro is still a Negro and can never muster the naturalized status of a United States Citizen; this decision has never been overturned, but in ex post facto concurrent tortfeasors of the subject. This irrelevancy of whether a Negro is a slave or free is reiterated in Section Four of the Fourteenth Amendment.

We sustain leadership among ourselves.

Due to long standing systems of education of our free status within the human family, while being shielded under the grandeur of feigned U.S. Citizenship, our nobility can now shine through the revised identifications of abolished Slave Labels. The abyss of slavery is evil and sinful when it has produced content slaves in the ignorance of knowing they are slaves. We have promoted, from the sons of Men, our equals to sovereign powers and set as rulers over ourselves, for the good of our Empire due to found freedom under nationalized citizenry.

The peace of all societies dependeth on Justice, the happiness of individuals, on the safe enjoyment of all their possessions, yet the so-called Black "Person" being a colorable American Citizen is itself possessed. The gold, silver and commerce belong to the citizens and because "all persons born or naturalized" are real property under the laws of the United States, so-called African Americans generate an annual 750 billion dollars as consumers yet have no true wealth and own no possessions as a people. Since it is not in the nature of chattel to also be the owner, the mass production of Negroes, Colored Folks and Black People made only in America was never designed for them to be autonomous themselves. From this die of court and State-owned Slavery alone, we had no rights that the true Citizens were bound to respect. We could never enjoy the peace of a society while latent in the perpetual Sin of Slavery.

Negroes, Blacks, and Colored People can not receive Divine Rights, unmolested by citizens. The granted privilege of the Negro Vote cannot be counted as 'one man one vote' while the '3/5

Clause' remain cloaked in the esoteric word 'Person' thereby rendering from a peopleless people the clandestine 'three-to-make-one' ballot at the discretion of the citizens to be cast hither, thither or where ever to favor their will.

Six score and fifteen years of post Slavery and emancipation of Moorish Nationals have not yielded their just Nationalization, Civilization, Reparations, nor Self-Education but depleted it for the economical, political, industrial, religious, befitting in the course of justice of the Moorish Americans to best honor the benevolence of that government through a Treaty of Peace and Friendship, rather than be a census tumor on the body of that State.

The colonies, corporations, towns, cities, homes, travel ways and means we have planted are our own. And our members shall enjoy the fruits of their labor in security and happiness consistent with the observance of our laws, the glory of our people shall be exalted to the world as products of our ingenuity.

We, as free Nationals, have our leaders call together the wise men of our people, to consult among them with freedom and hearth the opinion of them all, our magistrate are just, our ministers are wise. Families with land, wealth and autonomy can smile upon the flourishings of our arts, and gain strength from the science improved beneath the culture of our hands to be inherited by our sons and daughters.

The U.S. Administrative Government confounds the historical die of a slave-weakened people into illustrious 'Black History,' that severs us from the worthiness of our ancient forefathers and ostracizes us from the Family of Nations and the Human Family from whence we the Moorish are the founders and they derived. Now apology, gratitude and compensation is to be paid to those survivors of 400 years of slavery in America, the later 225 years of which were under the American flag.

Our system of education is steeped in Moro-Nationalism and surface degrees of character of color. Religion, forced upon slaves during the time of slavery, yielded an observance of a God that is nor our own nor graced with the Divine National freedom of We, as a Pure and Clean People. Our system of religion and education are squared to perpetuate our true image and likeness through adherence to our accomplishments and contributions to civilization prevalent to promote our generations.

Therefore, We, the representatives of the Clean and Pure Nation, including but not exclusively to, all families and tribes of Beys and Els in assembly of the Great Grand Body, under the Protection, Guidance and Salvation of the Great God of our Ancient Forefathers, Master of the Day of Judgment, for the resolution in the intent of our actions, do in our Free National Name, publicly Proclaim and Declare that We are an Anointed People, and of right are, Free, Upright and Autonomous.

The Moorish Americans as a Clean and Pure Nation have neither debts to the United States, her allies, enemies nor any nation neither foreign nor domestic to the North American Continent. We owe no obligations, economically, socially nor politically, for all are, the Evergreens, planted atop our shallow grave of perpetuated state of mental slavery here in the northwestern hemisphere. Indeed, our only atonement is to the Creator of all the Universe, both the Ruler and the Rich. For these reasons the Moorish Americans, having been forgiven for everything done wrong prior to the advent of our Founder Prophet, the Illustrious Noble Drew Ali, is hereby and henceforth a Clean and Pure Nation.

But, THE CORPORATE UNITED STATES remains greatly indebted to the Moors, with compounded interest, beginning with the magnanimous financial support from our Sultan in Morocco without which the United States would not have won Her independence, spurring America's first and oldest Treaty, through four hundred years of slave labor, to the industrial, medical, arts and scientific contributions, which She would not exist without the generations of Moorish staple. Nevertheless, the United States, in the initial post-slavery years, sustained the ex-slaves in a state of Mental Slavery and impecunious has not made an official apology or compensatory effort. Whereas reparations are never paid to Slaves, which would only perpetuate their present state of slavery, satisfactory compensation is always due to Surviving Hostages of the Nation that has endured the Maafa of African Slave Trade, Genocide, Denationalization, and Apartheid. The Moorish Americans have risen from the dust and is now that especial Nation.

The time is nigh and the fires of the prophesy are upon us. And according to the Divine Scheme of Human Events we are to let all old business stay as it is and do all our new business in the Free National Name of Moorish American. We, the vanguard tribes of the Moorish hordes in America, do hereby pray the following remedies be honored by the United States Supreme Court, the Executive Branch or/and and adept Special Congressional Committee, or other National or International authorized designated bodies to:

- Recognize the Free National Name, Number and Religious autonomy of the Moorish Americans as the Clean and Pure Nation with our Government, Religion, Officials, Flag, Seals, et al, in the glory of a Proper Person.
- To make into law an agreed fifty year indigenous people Mandate from which to purge into realization the Clean and Pure Nation of Moorish Americans within the security of The Moorish Science Temple of America, to acknowledge by revisions of the U.S. Laws that there are now and henceforth two new Nations brought forth on this Continent to live in harmony from the breast of one mother.
- To authenticate all necessary credentials for recognizing our Sheiks, Grand Sheiks, Governors, Grand Governors, as National Representatives and firmly establish a perpetual communication for our securities.
- To honor and preserve our Treaty of Peace and Friendship based upon the High Principles of Love, Truth, Peace, Freedom, and Justice. A perpetual Treaty with Acts to strengthen the National Securities of these Friendly Americas.
- To place into law all rights of Diplomatic Immunities, International Conveyance Authorization, secured lodging and the protection to peacefully co-exist in America, in harmony with the Divine Constitution and By-Laws of the Moorish Science Temple of America.
- An agreement to reside in all areas and well defined territories, previously civilized and settled by the Moors of Western Africa during the pre- and post-Columbian millenniums to prosper unmolested within North America.

- To call aloud the indigenous citizens of the United States of America, Allies, and Foreign Sympathizers to help us, the Free National Moorish Americans, economically, politically, socially, religiously, in our gigantic National and Divine Movement, the Uplifting of fallen humanity. We, as a Clean and Pure Nation, do not have enemies, foes, or adversaries nor do we possess the intent to create their likes from among the Sons of Man.

With these intents, THE PEOPLE OF THE UNITED STATES OF AMERICA and our greatness will be divinely assured and the Negro problem, which had become a great sin upon the earth will be finally and wholly solved. Only the Moorish Americans must rightfully proclaim this, their National and Divine Identification, hereby notifying the United States of America and all nations of the earth with the following Divine Constitution and By-Laws.

We, as an organic people, declaring our Free National Moorish American Autonomy must now proclaim:

> Our God is The Great God, The One Creator. Allah is this name in Arabia;
> Our Founding Father and Patriot is the Holy Prophet, Noble Drew Ali;
> Our National Pledge of Allegiance is the Moorish American Prayer;
> Our Constitution is The Divine Constitution and By-Laws of the M.S.T. of A.;
> Our Flag is a red flag with a five-pointed green star in the center;
> Our Grand National Symbol is The Logos Circle Seven;
> Our Grand National Emblem is The Crescent Moon and Star, Last Quarter;
> Our Principles are Love, Truth, Peace, Freedom, and Justice, Unity and Salvation;
> Our Government is Islamic with the Holy Koran as our Laws and Guide;
> Our Citizens are Moorish Americans, all bearing one Free National Name;
> Our Land upon the Earth shall be known as Amexem;
> Our President is The Supreme Grand Sheik;
> Our Vice President is The Supreme Grand Governor;
> Our Congressional Cabinet is a Grand Body of Grand Sheiks and Grand Governors;
> Our Supreme Court is The Supreme Grand Council;
> Our purpose is the Uplifting of fallen humanity;
> Our Gross National Product is Wisdom;
> Our International Prayer is the Al-Fatiha.

The Covenant of Allah is to Honor thy Father and thy Mother that thy days may be long upon the earthland, which the Lord thy God-Allah hath given thee. All Moorish Americans need to learn to love instead of hate and to know of their Higher Self and Lower Self. This is the uniting of Asia, the embodiment of the human family and the Great Quran of Mohammad. We are linking ourselves with the families of nations. We honor all true and divine Prophets, Jesus, Mohammad, Buddha, Confucius, and Ali.

Prophet makes a plea to nation

Our Divine and National Movement stands for the specific grand principles of Love, Truth, Peace, Freedom, and Justice, and I, the Prophet am applying to all loyal, faithful Moors, members, and the American citizens to help me in my great uplifting acts of uplifting fallen humanity among the Asiatic race and nation; for I have suffered much and severely in the past through misunderstanding of what the movement was dedicated to.

It is the Great God Allah alone that guides the destiny of this Divine and National Movement. I know all true American citizens are identified by national descent names to answer and apply to the free national constitution of this free National Republic of the United States of America. That's why I am calling on all true and national citizens to help me morally and financially in my great work I am doing to help this national government. For without a free national name, with a descent flag of your forefathers, there is not a national divine title of the government in which we live.

This is from your true and Divine Prophet unto all American and foreign sympathizers.

Prophet Noble Drew Ali

Salvation

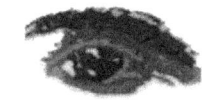
Allah

Unity

The Moorish Science Temple of America

THE DIVINE CONSTITUTION AND BY-LAWS

Act 1: The Grand Sheik and the chairman of the Moorish Science Temple of America is in power to make law and enforce laws with the assistance of the Prophet and the Grand Body of the Moorish Science Temple of America. The Assistant Grand Sheik is to assist the Grand Sheik in all affairs if he lives according to Love, Truth, Peace, Freedom, and Justice, and it is known before the members of the Moorish Science Temple of America.

Act 2: All meetings are to be opened and closed promptly according to the Circle Seven and Love, Truth, Peace, Freedom, and Justice. Friday is our Holy Day of rest, because on a Friday the first man was formed in flesh and on a Friday the first man departed out of flesh and ascended unto his father God, Allah, for that cause Friday is the Holy Day for all Moslems all over the world.

Act 3: Love, Truth, Peace, Freedom, and Justice must be proclaimed and practiced by all members of the Moorish Science Temple of America. No member is to put in danger or accuse falsely his brother or sister on any occasion at all that may harm his brother or sister, because Allah is Love.

Act 4: All members must preserve these Holy and Divine laws, and all members must obey the laws of the government, because by being a Moorish American, you are a part and parcel of the government, and must live the life accordingly.

Act 5: This organization of the Moorish Science Temple of America is not to cause any confusion or to overthrow the laws and constitution of the said government but to obey hereby.

Act 6: With us all members must proclaim their nationality and we are teaching our people their nationality and their divine creed that they may know that they are a part and a parcel of this said government, and know that they are not Negroes, Colored Folks, Black People, or Ethiopians, because these names were given to slaves by slave holders in 1779 and lasted until 1865 during the time of slavery, but this is a new era of time now, and all men now must proclaim their free national name to be recognized by the government in which they live and the nations of the earth, this is the reason why Allah the Great God of the universe ordained Noble Drew Ali, the Prophet to redeem his people from their sinful ways. The Moorish Americans are the descendants of the ancient Moabites whom inhabited the North Western and South Western shores of Africa.

Act 7: All members must promptly attend their meetings and become a part and a parcel of all uplifting acts of the Moorish Science Temple of America. Members must pay their dues and keep in line with all necessities of the Moorish Science Temple of America, then you are entitled to the name of "Faithful." Husband, you must support your wife and children; wife, you must obey your husband and take care of your children and look after the duties of your household. Sons and daughters must obey father and mother and be industrious and become a part of the uplifting of fallen humanity. All Moorish Americans must keep their hearts and minds pure with love, and their bodies clean with water. This Divine Covenant is from your Holy Prophet Noble Drew Ali, through the guidance of his Father God Allah.

Noble Drew Ali
Founder

MOORISH AMERICAN PRAYER

Allah the Father of the universe, the Father of Love, Truth, Peace, Freedom and Justice. Allah is my protector, my guide, and my salvation by night and by day, through his Holy Prophet Drew Ali. "Amen."

THE MOORISH SCIENCE TEMPLE OF AMERICA

Home Office: 57th & Federal St. Chicago, IL U.S.A.

The Proclaimed Members of the M.S.T. of A. and Nationalized Citizens of the U.S.A.

This Proclamation is therefore coming forth by day of a Nation of People being divinely brought forth into being. The "I Am" gnosis of reattaching ourselves, through the heritage and national descent of our Ancient Forefathers, to the Family of Nations, is the Rightful and Lawful Proclaiming of our free National Name, by descent and aboriginal/ indigenous live birth. Thereby a Proclamation of true and free National Status of Autonomy and inalienable Rights of Freedom including Religious liberty, endowed by the Great God of the Universe that created all men and women, sounding that trumpet aloud to all nations of the Earth, upon the hedges and highways, that the Moorish American have risen from the dust of Northwest America and neither will be harmed in the horizon of their coming forth by day.

Each living member of every family, desiring their unity and ours in this great purging of Sin and Crime in North America, has proclaimed aloud their nationality as Moorish Americans, Citizens of the U.S.A. via our Divine Prophet, Noble Drew Ali, Home Office, Chicago Illinois. Each member being a part and parcel of the whole, is autographed/ signed with the Moorish Tribal suffix "Bey" and "El," has officially attained the long promised Lost-Found Tribes of "Ali" and thereby breaking the old four-hundred year chain to the Slave labels of "Negro," "Black," "Colored," "African American," etc. Each Confirmation Certificate must be accompanied with the American State Certificate of Birth and Social Security Card etc. issued through the entitlements of U.S. Fourteenth Amendment, to be exchanged for a "Moorish American Nationality and Identification, Dues Card, Emergency Card, Per Capita Tax Card," to be valid.

This Proclamation is sent from the Moorish Science Temple California, Inc., Confirms Temple heads who have taken their seats in the affairs of nations.

PEACE.

MOORISH LEADER'S HISTORICAL MESSAGE TO AMERICA

In connection with the aims, objects, rules and regulations of the Moorish Science Temple of America, We deem it proper to submit to you a brief statement of our organization, covering its inception, rise, and progress and of the Mohammedan religion, which I hope will be satisfactory to you and be the means of causing you at all times to adhere to the principles of Love, Truth, Peace, Freedom, and Justice in your relations with mankind in general. I further, most anxiously hope this brief statement will help you more clearly see the duty and wisdom of at all times upholding those fundamental principles which are desired for our civilization of our posterity, such as obedience to law, respect, and loyalty to government, tolerance, and unity.

We organized as the Moorish Temple of Science in the year of 1925, and were legally incorporated as a civic organization under the laws of the State of Illinois, November 29th, 1926. The name Moorish Temple of Science changed to the Moorish Science Temple of America, May 1928, in accordance with the legal requirements of the Secretary of the State of Illinois.

The object of our Organization is to help in the great program of uplifting fallen humanity and teach those things necessary to make our members better citizens.

A National organization with a Rotarian complexion as it relates to branch Temples became obvious with the increasing number of inquiries from men and women in different sections of the country concerning the purpose of the organization. There are branch Temples in fifteen (15) different states at this time.

Since the work of the Moorish Science Temple of America was largely religious, the organization has been legally changed to a religious corporation and an affidavit to this effect has been properly filed in the Cook County Recorders office in Illinois.

Inspired by the lofty teachings of the Koran, we have it as the revealed word of God Allah. We shall foster the principles of its teachings among our members. This is our religious privilege as American citizens, under the laws of one of the greatest documents of all time-the American Constitution.

The Mohammedan religion is the least appreciated and probably the most misunderstood of the world's great religions. This is especially true in our western world. Try to understand what Mohammedanism stands for and some of the things it has contributed to the world.

Mohammed was the founder of the Mohammedan religion. It originated thirteen centuries ago on the Arabian Peninsula, where the streams of commerce and culture met and mingled in the middle ages, where the markets of exchange were stationed for treasures of India and the products of the Mediterranean coasts. There, this religion was established in the unprecedented short period of twenty years, and unlike many other religions, without the aid of any royal patronage and support. Buddhism had its Asoka; Judaism its Joshua; Christianity its Constantine; but Mohammedanism had no person of royal rank and power to assist in its establishment and spread.

Today this religion is acknowledged by nearly two hundred and fifty million souls and extends over an area equal to one-third of the globe. From Arabia it spread eastward over Persia, Turkestan, Afghanistan, westward across Syria, Asia Minor, Turkey; southward to Africa, covering more than half of that continent. It found its way to India, and beyond, to the Islands of Sumatra, Java, and Borneo.

To the early representative of this faith the world's debt is incalculably great. For it was they who transmitted the treasures of Greek literature from the middle ages to the Renaissance; they who originated the graceful forms of which the Taj Mahal and the Alhambra are the most famous examples. It was they who contributed to the sciences of algebra and chemistry, astronomy, and medicine; they who dotted the Saracen Empire with universities and who built at Bagdad and Cairo and most renowned universities of the world. During those centuries of ecclesiastical despotism when the Christian church suppressed all intellectual activities save those that were theological, causing the talent that reproduces to supplant the genius that creates. Mohammedans did all in their power to encourage and stimulate research in every branch of human inquiry.

The Moors or Mohammedans added to the beauty and grandeur of Spain. For centuries art, science, literature, and chivalry flourished among them, while the rest of Europe was still sunk in the gloom of the Dark Ages. The Moors were the most ingenious and industrious of the subjects of Spain. Their expulsion from Spain in 1610 was one of the chief causes of decadence of that country, for both agriculture and industry fell into decay after their departure.

Mohammedanism makes no distinction between high and low, rich and poor; it is like the sky, it has room for all.
The Koran should be of interest to all readers. It is the Bible of the Mohammedans, ruling over the customs and actions of over 200 million people. It is a work of importance whether considered from a religious, philosophical, or literary viewpoint.

In the promotion of plans for the betterment of mankind, there has ever been some kind of opposition. And strange as it may seem, such opposition has come from sources where there were no ideas or the lack of courage to force attention to ideas. Whether in a church, state or the social community, any attempt to do anything out of the usual way, seldom fails to receive criticism. Not because the course cannot be pursued legally or that it is unreasonable, but because it has been considered in terms as new.

The Moorish Science Temple of America has received some opposition and criticism. In the main the opposition has come from certain Christian ministers. They have expressed themselves as being opposed to our propagation of the Mohammedan religion. Possibly because the promotion of the Mohammedan faith among our people in the United States is considered by them in terms as something new. Whatever the reasons may be for their opposition, the legal right to oppose citizens, individuals and organizations alike for their religious belief does not exist in the United States. The door of religious freedom made by the American Constitution swings open to all, and people may enter through it and all worship as they desire. Without religious freedom, no search from truth would be possible; without religious freedom, no discovery of truth would be useful; without religious freedom, religious progress would be checked and we would no longer march forward towards the nobler life which the future holds for the races of men; without religious freedom, there would be no inspiration to lift our heads and gaze with a fearlessness into the vast beyond; seeking a hope eternal.

It is a sad weakness in us after all, to oppose our fellowmen for their religious beliefs, and if there are angels who record the sorrows of men as well as their sins, they certainly know how many and deep are the useless sorrows that spring forth from such opposition. Possibly, love and time will cancel our ancient hatreds in this regard and prove that in mankind, tolerance is better than unwarranted opposition.

In connection with our religious aims and beliefs, we must promote economic security. The preaching of economic security among us is by no means as widespread and intensive as the circumstances demand. No other one thing is more needed among us at this time than greater economic power. Better positions for our men and women, more business employment for our boys and girls and bigger incomes will follow our economic security. We shall be secure in nothing until we have economic power. A beggar people cannot develop the highest in them, nor can they attain to a genuine enjoyment of the spiritualities of life.

Our men, women and children should be taught to believe in the capacity of our group to succeed in business, in spite of the trials and failures of some of them. Trials and failures in business are by no means confined to any particular group of people. Some business ventures of all people fail. We have many men and women among our people who are qualified, both by training and experience, who are shining lights in the business world of all the people. It is a sad weakness in us as a people that we have withheld the very encouragement, support and patronage that would have made some of our worthy business ventures a grand success. And worst of all, have joined in the condemnations of them when they failed. Except in cases of actual dishonesty, discourtesy, lack of service, and actual unreliability, our business enterprises in every field of endeavor should have fullest of confidence cooperation and patronage whenever and wherever they can be given.

Read carefully the doctrines of the Moorish Science Temple of America. It contains our hopes, aims, rules, and articles of religion. Every member should have a copy.

In conclusion, I urge you to remember there is enough work for all to do in helping to build a better world. The problems of life are largely social and economic. In a profound sense, they are moral and spiritual. Have lofty conceptions of your duties to your country and fellowman in general and especially those with whom you deal. This includes such honesty and righteousness as will cause you to put yourself in the other fellow's place. Look for the best in others and give them the best that is in you. Have a deeper appreciation for womanhood. Brighten the hopes of your youth in order that their courage be increased to dare and do wondrous things. Adhere at all times to the principles of love, truth, peace, freedom, and justice.

I am your affectionate leader. I shall continue to labor day and night, both in public and private, for your good, thereby contributing to the welfare of our country and its people as a whole.

Prophet Noble Drew Ali

The Moorish Science Temple California, Inc.

Redondo Beach, California
califamoors@gmail.com

Online:
Google "Califa Media"
http://califamedia.com

FaceBook:
Califa Media

Twitter:
@califamedia

Official Full Color Version of This Text Available at CalifaMedia.com and Amazon.com

www.ingramcontent.com/pod-product-compliance
Lightning Source LLC
Chambersburg PA
CBHW081737100526
44591CB00016B/2645